THE LITTLE KERNEL COOKBOOK

BY PATRICIA STAPLEY

ILLUSTRATIONS BY JENNIE OPPENIIEIMER

CROWN PUBLISHERS, INC.
NEW YORK

For Nicholas

I wish to thank the following people for their help and support: Katharine Williams, Jill Benson, Joyce Jue, Judith Maas, Howard Rheingold, Jim Dutra, Christine Carswell, Svetlana Yakubovich, Aaron Stapley, Chuck Charlton, Esther Mitgang, and Rita Aero.

Published by Crown Publishers, Inc., 201 East 50th Street, New York, New York 10022. Member of the Crown Publishing Group.

CROWN is a trademark of Crown Publishers, Inc.

Manufactured in Hong Kong

Library of Congress Cataloging-in-Publication Data
Stapley, Patricia.
The little kernel cookbook / by Patricia Stapley; illustrations by Jennie Oppenheimer.
p. cm.
1. Cookery (Corn) I. Title
TX809.M2S73 1991
641.6'567--dc20   90-25077

ISBN 0-517-58355-0

10 9 8 7 6 5 4 3 2 1

FIRST EDITION

THE
LITTLE
KERNEL
COOKBOOK

CONTENTS

Introduction	**7**
Tuscan Salad with Olive and Polenta Triangles	**11**
Cavalry Corn Chowder with Popcorn Munitions	**14**
San Francisco Corn Crust Tie-Dyed Pizza	**17**
Sundance Corn Timbales with Pepper and Corn Relish	**21**
Sweet Corn Soufflé on a Compote of Country Peppers	**25**
Hominy-Stuffed Sweet Peppers on a Bed of Sweated Onions	**29**
Paris, Texas, Corn and Potato Pancakes	**32**
Floating Garden Corn and Crab Soup	**35**
Madras Corn Fritters with Chilled Cucumber Yogurt	**37**
Hearty Harvest Stew with White Corn Spoon Bread	**40**
Crusted Indian Corn Bake with Smoked Chilies	**45**
Flamenco Corn Gazpacho	**48**
Mardi Gras Corn Creole with Prawns on Parade	**51**
Santa Fe-Style Artichoke Enchiladas with Pipian Sauce	**54**
Aztec Onion and Lime Soup with Blue Corn Dumplings	**59**
Corn Blini Shortstack with Caviar Gorbachev	**62**

INTRODUCTION

The Little Kernel Cookbook is a celebration of one of the most delicious and versatile members of the plant kingdom. This marvelous plant — the only grain that is indigenous to North America — has become a unanimous favorite *and* an important staple in countries around the globe.

Surprisingly, corn is not merely a grain. It has the remarkable distinction of being a vegetable and a fruit as well. It is a healthful complex carbohydrate that is very low in fat and relatively high in fiber. It is also wonderfully low in calories, making it something of a miracle food, considering the taste it delivers.

Most of the recipes in *The Little Kernel Cookbook* call for sweet corn, and you can use corn that is freshly cut from the cob, fresh frozen, or canned. Either white or yellow corn is fine. One recipe includes hominy, a staple of the South and Central America. Hominy, made from kernels that are soaked and skinned, can be purchased canned in supermarkets. Another recipe calls for masa harina, which is dried hominy that is finely ground. Masa harina is used extensively in Mexican cooking, especially for corn tortillas, and is widely available in specialty food stores. A few of the recipes call for cornmeal, which is ground from dried fresh corn. Cornmeal

7

is available in white, yellow, or blue; the recipes will indicate which one to select. Corn flour, which is also called for, is very finely ground cornmeal. One of the recipes requires freshly popped popcorn.

When buying fresh corn, select ears with moist pale green stems and tightly wrapped green husks. When you peel back a husk, the kernels should be plump, even, and snug on the cob. My mother would pierce a kernel with her thumbnail, and if it squirted vigorously, she bought the ear. Her corn was always tender. If, out of season, you need fresh corn that crunches, you can buy frozen corn in kernels or on the cob.

Some recipes call for ultra-fresh corn, cut directly from the cob. To do this, stand the husked ear (with the silk removed) on its stem on a cutting board. Use a sharp knife to cut the kernels from top to bottom, three or four rows at a time. Cut close to the cob, and if some of the kernels stick together, leave them that way. It's a charming look, and demonstrates to your guests how fresh the corn really is.

If you do not plan to use your fresh ears of corn right away, leave the husks intact, put the ears in a plastic bag (leave it unsealed) and refrigerate them in the vegetable bin. When the husks start to dry out, the corn is old. You can also cut the kernels from fresh corn when you bring it home, and freeze them in plastic freezer bags or airtight containers. Or freeze whole ears by removing the husks and silk and wrapping the ears tightly in plastic freezer bags.

At the end of each recipe you will find a listing of the amounts of fiber, cholesterol, fat, and calories in each serving. Most recipes also have a "Lean Corn Tip" to help tailor them to saturated-fat- or cholesterol-restricted diets you or your guests may have, without sacrificing a bit of flavor in the wonderful meals you will be preparing.

As you savor these delicious recipes, keep in mind that this amazing golden grain will enhance your health while securing your reputation as an outstanding cook. Every recipe is a delight to create and, you will discover, a joy to share with your friends and loved ones.

Tuscan Salad
with Olive and Polenta
Triangles

Outdoor dining is an Italian tradition, and Tuscan Salad with Olive and Polenta Triangles creates the mood of al fresco dining at its very best. Golden, olive-studded polenta triangles combined with a tartly dressed fresh basil and spinach salad is a luncheon entree that sings of the hills overlooking Florence. Serve with saucers of extra-virgin olive oil for dipping hot, crusty Italian bread, and pour the wine for which Tuscany is renowned, Chianti.

Makes Six to Eight Servings

2 cups yellow cornmeal

7 to 8 cups cold water

1/2 teaspoon salt

3 tablespoons unsalted butter

1/2 cup grated pecorino Romano cheese

2 ounces black olives, pitted and sliced into thin rounds

2 ounces green olives, pitted and sliced into thin rounds

6 cups fresh spinach leaves, washed and drained

10 fresh basil leaves, washed and sliced

11

1/4 cup extra-virgin olive oil (plus a little extra, if
  necessary)
3 garlic cloves, minced
1/2 cup pine nuts
salt and freshly ground black pepper to taste
Parmesan cheese, freshly shaved or grated

Combine the cornmeal and seven cups of cold water in a large, heavy-bottomed saucepan. Mix well. Add the salt.

Cook the polenta over low heat for thirty minutes, stirring frequently. If the polenta becomes stiff and difficult to stir, add more cold water slowly. The polenta is done when the grain is a soft texture against your tongue.

Stir in the butter, Romano cheese, and olives. Mix well.

Pour the hot olive-studded polenta onto a buttered baking sheet and, with a spatula, spread it into a layer about seven inches wide and one inch thick. Let it set for thirty minutes.

When the polenta has cooled and firmed up, cut it into three-and-a-half-inch squares. Then cut the squares into triangles. (You will have about eighteen triangles.) Set aside.

Preheat the oven to 400 degrees.

Separate and arrange the polenta triangles in a single layer on the rebuttered baking sheet and bake for about ten minutes. They will become crusty and golden in color.

While the triangles are baking, combine the spinach and basil in a large salad bowl.

Heat the olive oil in a skillet over a moderate heat. Add the garlic and pine nuts and sauté for a minute or two, until lightly browned.

When the polenta triangles are done, arrange two or

three on the rim of each plate. Toss the salad with the warm dressing until the spinach leaves become glossy. Salt and pepper to taste. Put a generous portion on each plate, and serve immediately.

For the ultimate taste of Tuscany, shave the Parmesan cheese over the salads at the table.

Lean Corn Tip: Omit the butter and/or Romano cheese in the polenta, and the Parmesan cheese. Reduce the pine nuts to one-quarter cup. Use an unbuttered nonstick baking sheet.

Each Lean Corn serving contains:

> • FIBER: 1 GRAM • CHOLESTEROL: 0 MILLIGRAMS
> • FAT: 17 GRAMS • CALORIES: 309

Cavalry Corn Chowder
with
Popcorn Munitions

In the "Battle of Little Big Corn," the tame northeastern chowder is no match for this zesty southwestern version. Croutons of popcorn, fresh from the microwave, garnish the dish with surefire crunch. Cavalry Corn Chowder, served in festive deep bowls, creates a warm, informal mood for gatherings of family and friends. Complete this earthy offering with a crisp jicama salad, a frosty mug of beer, and pineapple upside-down cake.

Makes Six Servings

3 poblano or Anaheim chilies
8 ounces tomatillos, fresh or canned
3 cups corn kernels
1 cup water
2 tablespoons butter
1 medium onion, finely chopped
2 garlic cloves, minced
1 teaspoon salt
1/2 teaspoon freshly ground black pepper
3 cups milk
1 teaspoon chili powder

cilantro (fresh coriander) leaves, coarsely chopped,
for garnish
2 cups plain popped popcorn

Preheat the broiler.

Place the chilies under the broiler and turn them to char
on all sides. When the skins are thoroughly charred and the
flesh is softened, remove the chilies and put them in a plastic
or paper bag. Close the bag and leave the chilies to sweat for
ten minutes. Remove them from the bag, peel them, cut them
in half, and discard the seeds and stems. Dice the chilies and
set them aside.

If you are using fresh tomatillos, bring several cups of
water to a boil, then lower the heat to a simmer. Remove the
papery husks from the tomatillos, put them in the hot water,
and let them simmer slowly for ten minutes. Drain the tomatillos, transfer them to a food processor or blender, and
purée. (If you use canned tomatillos, drain them and then
purée.) Set the tomatillos aside.

In a food processor or blender, purée two cups of corn
kernels with a cup of water until smooth. Strain the corn
purée through a medium-mesh sieve to press out all of the liquid. Reserve the liquid and discard the pulp.

Melt the butter in a heavy-bottomed saucepan. Add the
onion and garlic and cook over medium-low heat until soft.
Add the chilies, tomatillo purée, salt, pepper, and the remaining cup of corn kernels, and sauté for two to three minutes.
Stir in the reserved corn liquid and milk, and continue to
cook over low heat for thirty minutes.

Ladle the chowder into oversized earthenware bowls.
Pottery in a southwestern pattern would be ideal. Sprinkle a

pinch of chili powder over one half of the surface of the chowder and sprinkle a bit of the cilantro over the other half. You now have a surface that is half red and half green. Sprinkle a small handful of popcorn kernels down the middle, where they will float on the surface like croutons.

Lean Corn Tip: Substitute olive oil for the butter, and low-fat milk for the whole milk.

Each Lean Corn serving contains:

- FIBER: 1.6 GRAMS • CHOLESTEROL: 5 MILLIGRAMS
- FAT: 6.8 GRAMS • CALORIES: 196

San Francisco
Corn Crust
Tie-Dyed Pizza

Let your imagination flow. Visualize a New Age pizza with a truly cosmic flavor. The cornmeal makes a fabulously golden, crunchy crust for your masterpiece. Flower children of the nineties will want to serve the pizzas out in the garden, with chilled bottles of Frascati, marinated mushrooms, and a salad of mixed greens — adorned, of course, with nasturtiums.

Makes Two Twelve-Inch Pizzas (Serves Four to Six)

1 package active dry yeast (2 1/2-ounces)
1 cup warm water
2 cups unbleached white flour
7 tablespoons olive oil (plus a little extra for oiling
    the dough and utensils)
1/2 teaspoon salt
1 cup yellow cornmeal
1/2 cup chopped fresh basil leaves
2 tablespoons grated Parmesan cheese
2 tablespoons chopped walnuts
1 tablespoon pine nuts
2 garlic cloves, crushed
8 ounces mozzarella cheese

1 medium onion, sliced paper thin
2 cups thinly sliced bright red and yellow tomatoes
1 orange bell pepper, cored, seeded, and thinly sliced
1 cup corn kernels

Preheat the oven to 500 degrees. To achieve the best results, a conventional home oven should be preheated for one hour.

In a large bowl, dissolve the yeast in warm water. Mix well. Add one and a half cups of the white flour and combine thoroughly. Add two tablespoons of the olive oil, the salt, and the remaining half cup of white flour. Gradually add the cornmeal, working the dough with your hands until all of the cornmeal is incorporated and the dough holds its shape.

Put the dough in an oiled large bowl and turn it once so that its surface becomes coated. Cover the bowl and let the dough rise in a warm place until it has doubled in size, about forty to forty-five minutes.

Meanwhile, make a pesto sauce by putting the basil, the remaining five tablespoons of olive oil, and the Parmesan, walnuts, pine nuts, and garlic in a food processor or blender. Blend until smooth. (Be sure the pesto isn't too thick to spoon onto the pizza; if it is, thin it with additional oil.)

Slice the mozzarella into sticks two and a half inches long by a quarter inch wide and deep. Set aside.

Assemble all of the other toppings — the onion, tomatoes, pepper, and corn. For best results, you will want to top your rolled dough without delay.

Oil two baking sheets, lightly dust them with flour, and then sprinkle the surface with a little cornmeal.

When the dough has doubled in size, divide it in two. Form each part into a ball with your hands and place it on a lightly floured surface.

The dough is now ready to be shaped, topped, and baked. With a lightly floured rolling pin, roll out each ball of dough to roughly twelve inches in diameter. The pizza should be about one eighth to a quarter inch thick. Don't worry about creating a perfectly round shape. A rustic round has a charming homemade look.

Transfer each pie to a floured baking sheet. Brush the surface with a little olive oil to ensure a crisp crust.

Top the pizzas with a layer of onions and then add artistic layers of the tomatoes, pepper, and corn kernels. As an essential tie-dye touch, make crisscrosses on top of the vegetables with the sticks of mozzarella.

Bake the pizzas for twelve to fifteen minutes, or until the edges and bottoms are well browned.

Remove the pizzas from the oven and transfer to two large flat plates. For the final psychedelic flourish, spoon the pesto in thin wavy lines over the surface of the pizzas. Cut into wedges and serve at once.

Lean Corn Tip: Use low-fat mozzarella.

Each Lean Corn serving contains:
- FIBER: 2 GRAMS • CHOLESTEROL: 40 MILLIGRAMS
- FAT: 25 GRAMS • CALORIES: 401

Sundance Corn Timbales with Pepper and Corn Relish

One of the exciting aspects of cooking with corn is its remarkable versatility. Sundance Corn Timbales give a nouvelle twist to a culinary classic. The flavors are assertive, the texture is soft, the presentation is inspired. Turn this entree into a memorable meal with such spirited accompaniments as black beans and rice, sparkling grapefruit coolers, and wild blackberry cobbler.

Makes Six Servings

4 tablespoons butter
1/4 cup minced onion
3 cups corn kernels
4 tablespoons finely chopped fresh parsley
3 tablespoons finely chopped cilantro (fresh
    coriander) leaves
4 eggs
1 cup grated sharp cheddar cheese
1/4 teaspoon cayenne pepper
dash of Tabasco sauce
3/4 cup unseasoned bread crumbs
Pepper and Corn Relish (recipe follows)

Preheat the oven to 325 degrees.

Melt two tablespoons of the butter in a skillet over medium-low heat. Add the onion and sauté for one minute. Add one cup of the corn kernels, the parsley, and the cilantro, and sauté for two more minutes. Remove the skillet from the heat.

In a food processor or blender, purée the remaining two cups of corn kernels to a fairly smooth consistency.

In a large bowl, beat the eggs well with a whisk. Stir in the corn purée. Then add the sautéed corn. Fold in the cheddar cheese, and season with cayenne and Tabasco.

Butter six one-cup ramekins or custard cups (or twelve half cups). Coat them evenly and thoroughly with the bread crumbs. Mix any remaining crumbs into the timbale batter.

Spoon the batter into the ramekins to three quarters full.

Arrange the ramekins in a roasting pan. Pour enough hot water into the pan to submerge the cups halfway. Set the pan in the oven and bake for about forty-five minutes, or until the tops of the timbales puff up and become browned.

Remove the timbales from the oven and let them cool for a few minutes before unmolding them. To unmold the timbales, invert the ramekins onto individual dinner plates. Run a butter knife around the edge of the timbale if it does not slip out easily on its own.

Serve the Sundance Corn Timbales topped and circled with the Pepper and Corn Relish. White china plates will best highlight this colorful dish.

Lean Corn Tip: In the corn timbales, replace the butter with olive oil and reduce the cheddar cheese to one-half cup. Use an egg substitute in place of the whole eggs.

Each Lean Corn serving contains:
- FIBER: 1 GRAM • CHOLESTEROL: 20 MILLIGRAMS
- FAT: 26 GRAMS • CALORIES: 435

Pepper and Corn Relish

The Pepper and Corn Relish will keep for a week stored in the refrigerator. It is an equally delicious condiment for grilled vegetables, fish, and meats.

Makes Two and One-Half Cups

1 small red bell pepper, cored and seeded
1 small green bell pepper, cored and seeded
1 cup corn kernels
1/4 cup finely chopped red onion
2 tablespoons finely chopped cilantro (fresh
    coriander) leaves
1/4 cup virgin olive oil
2 tablespoons balsamic vinegar
salt and freshly ground black pepper to taste

Cut the peppers into quarter-inch squares and combine them with the corn kernels, onion, and cilantro in a small ceramic or glass bowl. Add just enough of the olive oil to cover the ingredients, and season with the vinegar and salt and pepper. Toss to mix well, and marinate at room temperature for two hours.

Before you serve, drain off any excess oil.

Sweet Corn Soufflé on a Compote of Country Peppers

Your table will sparkle when you surprise your guests with this elegant corn creation. Perched light as a feather on a base of colorful peppers, the Sweet Corn Soufflé becomes a delicious Provençal entree when accompanied by warmed rosemary bread and a glass of crisp white Burgundy.

Makes Six Servings

SOUFFLÉ

> 2 eggs, at room temperature, separated
> 2 tablespoons butter
> 2 tablespoons all-purpose flour
> 1 cup milk
> 2 cups cooked corn kernels
> 1 teaspoon salt
> 1/4 teaspoon freshly ground black pepper

COMPOTE

> 4 medium sweet bell peppers (2 red and 2 green)
> 3 tablespoons olive oil
> 3 shallots, minced
> 5 garlic cloves, minced

1 cup dry white wine
1/4 teaspoon herbes de Provence
salt and freshly ground black pepper to taste

Preheat the oven to 350 degrees.

Put the egg yolks in a small bowl and beat them thoroughly. Set aside.

In a medium saucepan, melt one tablespoon of butter over moderate heat. Sprinkle in the flour, stirring constantly. Cook for two minutes. Add the milk slowly, and continue to stir for about two minutes, until the liquid thickens to the consistency of sour cream.

One at a time, stir several tablespoons of the hot milk mixture into the bowl of beaten egg yolks. (This warms the yolks gradually and prevents them from cooking too swiftly.) Then pour the contents of the bowl into the saucepan of hot milk mixture. Stir and cook for one minute longer. Remove the pan from the heat. Add the corn kernels, salt, and pepper, and stir to combine. Transfer the batter to a large bowl.

Beat the egg whites until they are stiff and form soft peaks. Gently fold one quarter of the whites into the corn batter. Then add the remaining whites, delicately folding them into the batter with a rubber spatula. Turn the bowl as you fold. Remember, the egg whites ensure a light airy texture to the soufflé, so be careful to preserve the fluffiness as you fold.

Grease a one-and-a-half-quart casserole or soufflé dish with the remaining tablespoon of butter. Pour the batter into the casserole and bake for about thirty to thirty-five minutes. Do not open the oven door while the soufflé is baking. When the soufflé is done the crown will rise and turn a golden color.

As the soufflé cooks, prepare the pepper compote. Core,

seed, and dice the peppers.

Heat the olive oil in a medium saucepan over moderate heat. Add the shallots and garlic and sauté for three minutes. Then add the peppers. Cook and stir for five minutes. Pour in the wine, bring to a boil, and season with the herbes de Provence and salt and pepper to taste. Pour the compote into a bowl and let it cool while the soufflé is baking.

As soon as the soufflé is removed from the oven, spread the pepper compote on six French country-style dishes. At the table, scoop out generous portions of soufflé and serve it atop the compote. *Bon appétit.*

Lean Corn Tip: Substitute corn oil for the butter when greasing the soufflé dish. Replace the whole milk with low-fat milk.

Each Lean Corn serving contains:

• FIBER: 1 GRAM • CHOLESTEROL: 101 MILLIGRAMS
• FAT: 13 GRAMS • CALORIES: 285

Hominy-Stuffed Sweet Peppers on a Bed of Sweated Onions

It's the golden nuggets of hominy inside these glossy peppers that give them their uniquely scrumptious flavor and texture. One bite and you'll understand why hominy is the South's premier comfort food. On a cold autumn day, Hominy-Stuffed Sweet Peppers on a Bed of Sweated Onions is the ideal lap-top supper around the living-room fireplace. Complement this down-home fare with a salad of garden greens dressed with a squeeze of lemon and a drizzle of olive oil.

Makes Six Servings

6 large yellow onions
3 tablespoons butter
salt and freshly ground black pepper to taste
6 medium sweet bell peppers (preferably a colorful
    combination of red, yellow, green, orange,
    purple)
3 tablespoons olive oil
4 cups yellow hominy, or 2 16-ounce cans
1 or 2 fresh serrano chilies, seeded and minced
4 tomatoes, peeled and coarsely chopped
1/4 cup minced fresh parsley

1/4 cup chopped fresh basil leaves
1 teaspoon salt
1/2 teaspoon freshly ground black pepper
2 cups unseasoned bread crumbs

Preheat the oven to 350 degrees.

Begin by sweating the onions. Select a heavy-bottomed skillet with a lid. Cut a circle of foil about two inches wider than the diameter of the lid. Grease one side of the foil with a tablespoon of butter. Thinly slice five of the onions and separate them into rings. Melt the remaining two tablespoons of butter in the skillet and add the onion rings. Spread them out evenly and season to taste with salt and pepper. Place the greased foil loosely over the skillet and jam on the lid. Gently simmer the onions for forty to forty-five minutes. When they are done they will be very soft and appear transparent. Their flavor will be quite sweet.

While the onions are cooking, prepare the bell peppers by cutting off the tops and removing the seeds. Plunge them into a large pot of boiling water and cook them for two minutes. Drain them and set aside.

Finely chop the last onion. Heat two tablespoons of olive oil in a second skillet and add the chopped onion, the hominy, and the chilies. Sauté for about three minutes, stirring occasionally. Remove the mixture from the skillet to a bowl and add the tomatoes, parsley, basil, salt, pepper, and one cup of bread crumbs. Mix well to combine.

Using the remaining one tablespoon of olive oil, grease a shallow baking dish large enough to hold the bell peppers without crowding. Loosely stuff each pepper with the filling mixture, almost to the top. Sprinkle the remaining one cup of bread crumbs over the stuffed peppers.

Bake the peppers for thirty to forty minutes, or until the crumb tops are lightly browned.

Arrange the colorful stuffed peppers in a circle on a large round platter and fill the center with the sweated onions. Let your guests create a bed of onions on their own plates, topped with a pepper.

Lean Corn Tip: Substitute olive oil for the butter used to sweat the onions.

Each Lean Corn serving contains:

- FIBER: 3 GRAMS • CHOLESTEROL: 0 MILLIGRAMS
- FAT: 14 GRAMS • CALORIES: 363

Paris, Texas, Corn and Potato Pancakes

For a casual Wild West dinner, pull on your blue jeans and start smoldering a down-home barbecue sauce to add zest to every crunchy bite. Spread your table in the great outdoors with a brightly checkered cloth, and serve baby squash (sautéed or steamed, you choose) with the blossoms still flowering.

Makes Eighteen to Twenty Pancakes (Serves Six)

5 medium potatoes
1 cup corn kernels
1 small onion, grated
2 tablespoons corn flour
2 teaspoons baking powder
1 egg, beaten
salt and freshly ground black pepper to taste
4 tablespoons corn oil

Peel the potatoes. Using the medium blade of a grater, grate them into a colander. When you have made a mound of grated potatoes, empty the colander onto a cloth dish towel. Gather the ends of the towel in one hand, and with the other hand twist and squeeze the bundle of grated potatoes to wring out as much liquid as you can. Put the grated potato in a large bowl and set aside.

In a food processor or blender, purée half a cup of the corn kernels. Add the corn purée and onion to the potatoes. Add the corn flour, baking powder, egg, and salt and pepper. Mix well to combine.

Heat a large skillet to medium temperature. Oil the bottom of the skillet and warm it over the heat. Toss in the remaining half cup of corn kernels. Sauté the kernels for one to two minutes and salt and pepper to taste. Remove the corn to a bowl and set aside.

Reheat the skillet over medium heat and add more oil. When the oil becomes hot, drop about two tablespoons of the batter into the skillet and shape it with a spatula into a flat pancake about three and a half inches in diameter. Continue making pancakes until the pan is full. Be sure not to crowd the pancakes, or they will become soggy. Sauté over medium heat for approximately three minutes, or until the bottoms are crisp and brown. Turn them over and brown the other side, about three minutes. Transfer the pancakes to an oven-proof serving dish and keep them warm in a low oven while you continue to make batches of pancakes.

Arrange the pancakes on a Texas-sized platter and garnish with the sautéed corn kernels. Serve hot, with a spicy barbecue sauce right nearby.

Lean Corn Tip: Use a nonstick skillet and reduce the amount of corn oil from four tablespoons to two. Replace the egg with egg substitute.

Each Lean Corn serving contains:

• FIBER: 1 GRAM • CHOLESTEROL: 0 MILLIGRAMS
• FAT: 9 GRAMS • CALORIES: 198

Floating Garden Corn and Crab Soup

Tender crab meat, fresh young corn, and delicate ribbons of egg weave silken flavor into this classic soup from Thailand. Wonderfully easy to prepare, Floating Garden Corn and Crab Soup is enchanting when served in celadon bowls with porcelain spoons. Transform this single dish meal into a Siamese banquet with a smoked trout and watercress salad and a sparkling glass of iced lemongrass tea.

Makes Four Servings

2 scallions, green tops only, for garnish
1 tablespoon peanut oil
5 garlic cloves, minced
3 shallots, minced
3 cups chicken stock
2 tablespoons nam pla (fish sauce, available at
    specialty food shops)
8 ounces crab meat, cooked and shredded
1 cup corn kernels
1/2 teaspoon cracked black peppercorns
1 egg, beaten
1 radish, trimmed and sliced paper thin, for garnish

2 tablespoons cilantro (fresh coriander) leaves, for
   garnish
1 tablespoon finely grated lemon zest, for garnish

Wash the scallion tops and slice them into strips a quarter
inch wide by two inches long. Tie a loose knot in the middle
of each strip. Place the knotted scallions in a small bowl of ice
water. Set them aside to curl.

In a large saucepan, heat the oil over medium heat.
Sauté the garlic and shallots until soft but not browned. Add
the chicken stock, nam pla, crab meat, corn kernels, and peppercorns. Turn up the heat and bring to a boil.

Stirring constantly, slowly pour in the beaten egg.
Almost immediately, it will form lacy ribbons. As soon as the
egg is cooked, lower the heat and let the soup simmer for
three minutes. If you are using canned or frozen corn, simmer the soup for one minute only.

Drain the scallions.

Pour the steaming-hot soup into a wide tureen or, if you
prefer, into individual bowls. Carefully arrange a floating garden of garnish on the surface of the soup — the curly scallions, radish slices, whole cilantro leaves, and grated lemon.

Lean Corn Tip: Instead of one whole egg, use the whites of
two eggs.

Each Lean Corn serving contains:
   • FIBER: .5 GRAMS • CHOLESTEROL: 30 MILLIGRAMS
      • FAT: 14.6 GRAMS • CALORIES: 190

Madras Corn Fritters with Chilled Cucumber Yogurt

Impress your guests with a festive Indian extravaganza — serve Madras Corn Fritters with Chilled Cucumber Yogurt as the centerpiece of a *thali*. Arrange the mouth-watering fritters in the heart of individual platters. Surround them with sumptuous helpings of Chilled Cucumber Yogurt, basmati rice, curried vegetables, and a selection of chutneys. Pots of aromatic cardamom spiced tea and slices of the juiciest mango for dessert will add the finishing touches to a dinner fit for a rajah.

Makes Sixteen Fritters (Serves Four or Five)

1 cup all-purpose flour
1 teaspoon baking powder
2 eggs, beaten
2 cups corn kernels
2 scallions, green tops included, chopped
1 teaspoon minced garlic
1 tablespoon grated or finely chopped fresh ginger
    root
1 to 2 green chilies, seeded and minced
1 teaspoon ground cumin
1 teaspoon ground coriander

1 teaspoon ground turmeric
1 teaspoon salt
1/4 cup peanut oil
Chilled Cucumber Yogurt (recipe follows)

Sift the flour with the baking powder into a medium-sized bowl. Mix in the eggs and then fold in the corn kernels. Add the scallions, garlic, ginger, chilies, cumin, coriander, turmeric, and salt. Mix well, but gently, to combine.

In a heavy-bottomed medium-sized skillet, heat two tablespoons of the oil over medium heat. (The oil should not be too hot or the fritters will brown too quickly on the outside, leaving the inside undercooked.)

Drop the batter into the oil, a tablespoon at a time, to make fritters about two inches in diameter. Be careful not to crowd the skillet. Fry the fritters for about two minutes, until golden. Turn them over and fry for another minute and a half, or until the fritters are browned and firm on both sides.

Remove the fritters from the skillet and lay them on paper towels to soak up any excess oil. Keep them hot in a warm oven. Repeat the process for the remaining fritters, adding more oil to the pan, if necessary, for each batch.

Lean Corn Tip: In the Madras Corn Fritters, substitute three egg whites for the two whole eggs. In the Chilled Cucumber Yogurt, replace the whole yogurt and sour cream with one and a half cups of nonfat yogurt.

Each Lean Corn serving contains:
- FIBER: 1.3 GRAMS • CHOLESTEROL: 2.4 MILLIGRAMS
- FAT: 23 GRAMS • CALORIES: 414

Chilled Cucumber Yogurt

Let the Cucumber Yogurt chill for an hour before serving.

Makes Two Cups

> 2 medium cucumbers
> 1 medium tomato
> 1 cup plain yogurt
> 1/2 cup sour cream
> 2 tablespoons finely chopped fresh mint leaves
> 1/2 teaspoon salt

Peel the cucumbers and cut them in half lengthwise. Scrape the seeds out and discard them. Using the coarse side of a grater, shred the cucumbers into a ceramic or glass bowl.

Cut the tomato into quarters, core, and remove the seeds. Slice the tomato into thin strips, and combine with the cucumbers. Add the yogurt, sour cream, mint, and salt. Stir to mix thoroughly. Chill in the refrigerator.

Hearty Harvest Stew with White Corn Spoon Bread

Hearty Harvest Stew is an American classic. This southern-style version — seasoned with a shot of bourbon and topped with a melt-in-your-mouth mound of corn spoon bread — introduces the gracious warmth of the old South to a special circle of friends. Serve with a tall cool glass of pink lemonade spiked with a sprig of fresh mint. And don't forget that all-American apple pie topped with ice cream.

Makes Six Servings

HARVEST STEW

1 tablespoon unsalted butter
1 tablespoon olive oil
1 large onion, chopped
1 garlic clove, chopped
1 tablespoon all-purpose flour
1/2 teaspoon salt
1/4 teaspoon freshly ground black pepper
1/4 teaspoon allspice
1/8 teaspoon mace
3 cups chicken or vegetable stock

2 medium tomatoes, coarsely chopped (or substitute
   one 14-ounce can Italian tomatoes, drained and
   chopped)
1 medium turnip, peeled and cut into 1/2-inch slices
3 medium carrots, peeled and cut into 1/2-inch slices
2 medium potatoes, peeled and cubed
8 ounces small okra, cut into 1/2-inch slices
1 cup corn kernels
2 tablespoons bourbon
several pinches of cayenne pepper

SPOON BREAD

1 cup white cornmeal
1 1/2 cups water
1 tablespoon butter, melted
3 eggs, separated
1 cup buttermilk
1 teaspoon salt
1 teaspoon sugar
1 teaspoon baking powder
1/4 teaspoon baking soda

Heat the butter with the oil in a large heavy pot over medium heat. Add the onion and sauté until wilted. Add the garlic and sauté until soft. Sprinkle in the flour, salt, pepper, allspice, and mace, and continue to cook, stirring constantly, for two minutes.

Add the stock, scraping the bottom and sides of the pot with a wooden spoon. Stir in the tomatoes, and let the broth come to a low boil.

Add the turnip, carrots, potatoes, and okra. Lower the

heat, cover the pot, and simmer gently for about forty minutes, or until the vegetables are tender.

Meanwhile, preheat the oven to 375 degrees.

Butter a two-quart casserole or eight-by-ten-inch baking dish.

Place the cornmeal in a large bowl. Bring the water to a boil and pour it over the cornmeal, stirring constantly so that no lumps form. Add the melted butter, egg yolks, buttermilk, salt, sugar, baking powder, and baking soda, and beat until well blended.

Beat the egg whites until they stand in soft peaks. Gently fold them into the cornmeal mixture.

Pour the batter into the casserole and bake for about thirty minutes, or until the center is dry and the top is lightly browned and puffed.

About five minutes before the spoon bread is due to come out of the oven, add the corn kernels, bourbon, and cayenne to the stew. Stir well to combine. Keep the stew warm over very low heat until the spoon bread is puffed and golden.

Ladle the stew into warmed individual serving bowls. Let your guests serve themselves the hot-from-the-oven White Corn Spoon Bread. Like a dumpling, a generous mound should float atop each bowl.

Lean Corn Tip: In the Hearty Harvest Stew, omit the butter and increase the olive oil to two tablespoons. In the Spoon Bread, replace the butter with corn oil (and use corn oil to grease the dish), and replace the buttermilk with low-fat milk.

Each Lean Corn serving contains:

- FIBER: 1.5 GRAMS • CHOLESTEROL: 152 MILLIGRAMS
- FAT: 8 GRAMS • CALORIES: 218

Crusted Indian
Corn Bake
with Smoked Chilies

Crusted Indian Corn Bake with Smoked Chilies is a seasonal casserole that celebrates the rich tradition of Native American cuisine. This cornucopia of the late autumn harvest combines potatoes, leeks, and the last fresh corn of the season. The Indians call corn "maize," which means "life," and they have created hundreds of dishes from this American grain. To capture the mood of autumn, decorate your table with candlelight and a multicolored centerpiece of ornamental dried corn and squash. A green salad, sprinkled with walnuts and a gingered pumpkin pie with fresh whipped cream make wonderful accompaniments.

Makes Four Servings

5 dried chilies, smoked (available in specialty food
    shops)
3 medium leeks, white parts only
1 fennel bulb
6 small red potatoes
2 cups corn kernels
1 garlic clove, crushed
salt and freshly ground black pepper to taste

45

1/2 cup heavy cream
3 tablespoons butter
1 cup dry cornbread stuffing

Soak the chilies in hot water for about five minutes, until they are rehydrated and softened. Drain and coarsely chop them. Set aside.

Slice the leeks into quarter-inch rounds and wash them well. Set them aside in a large bowl.

Quarter the fennel bulb, trim away the core, and cut the fennel lengthwise into slices one quarter inch thick. Combine with the leeks.

Peel the potatoes and slice them into rounds one eighth inch thick. Add them to the bowl of leeks and fennel.

Preheat the oven to 375 degrees.

Butter the bottom and sides of an nine-by-nine-inch baking dish or a two-quart casserole. Rub the inside of the dish with the crushed garlic.

Lay half the vegetables in the baking dish, sprinkle with half the chilies, and season with salt and pepper. Pour in a quarter cup of the cream. Repeat with the remaining ingredients to form a second layer: add the vegetables, sprinkle the chilies, season with salt and pepper, and pour in the other quarter cup of cream.

Loosely cover the top of the dish with tinfoil, and cook for thirty minutes.

While the casserole is baking, melt the butter in a medium saucepan. Remove the pan from the heat and mix in the cornbread crumbs to coat them with the butter.

After the Corn Bake has cooked for thirty minutes, remove it from the oven. Take off the foil and cover the surface with the cornbread crumbs.

Return the Crusted Indian Corn Bake to the oven and continue baking, uncovered, until the vegetables are tender and the crusty top is browned, about thirty minutes.

Let the Crusted Indian Corn Bake cool for ten minutes before bringing it to the table. Serve this earthy offering family style. Your guests will enjoy helping themselves.

Lean Corn Tip: Substitute whole milk for the heavy cream. Use margarine instead of butter.

Each Lean Corn serving contains:

- FIBER: 4.9 GRAMS • CHOLESTEROL: 1 MILLIGRAM
- FAT: 9 GRAMS • CALORIES: 358

Flamenco
Corn
Gazpacho

This classic soup of Spain — with a sun-ripened twist — simply bursts with the flavors of fresh garden vegetables. Welcome your guests with savory tapas and chilled white Rioja. Contrast the tangy gazpacho with a salad of Valencia oranges and toasted pecans. This easy, make-ahead meal can create a midnight supper as lively as the streets of Seville.

Makes Six Servings

2 cups fresh corn kernels, cut from the cob
2 1/2 cucumbers, peeled and chopped
5 ripe medium tomatoes, peeled and chopped
2 shallots, chopped
3 tablespoons chopped fresh basil leaves
1 red bell pepper, cored, seeded, and chopped
1 onion, chopped
4 slices French bread, crusts removed
1 1/2 cups cold water
1/4 cup red wine vinegar
salt and freshly ground black pepper to taste
1/4 teaspoon cayenne pepper
1/4 cup plus 2 tablespoons extra-virgin olive oil

1 garlic clove, peeled and cut in half
1/2 green pepper, cored, seeded, and finely diced,
    for garnish

Set aside half a cup of the corn kernels and half a cup of the chopped cucumber.

In a deep bowl, combine the remaining corn kernels and cucumber with the tomatoes, shallots, basil, red pepper, and onion. Shred two slices of French bread into large, bite-size pieces and add to the vegetables. With a wooden spoon, stir in the water, vinegar, salt and black pepper, and cayenne.

In a food processor or blender, briefly process the vegetable mixture in small batches. Do not process it too long. The corn gazpacho should retain some raw vegetable crunch.

Pour the corn gazpacho into a large earthenware tureen. With a whisk, blend in the quarter cup of olive oil. Cover the bowl, and chill the soup for at least two hours.

Grill the remaining two slices of bread under a broiler just until they begin to brown. The bread should remain soft inside. Remove the slices from broiler and, while the bread is still hot, rub them with the cut side of the garlic. Brush them front and back with the remaining olive oil. Cut the bread into half-inch cubes to make garlic croutons. Set aside.

When you are ready to serve your guests, stir the gazpacho, taste it, and correct the seasoning if necessary. Ladle it into chilled bowls. For the colorful garnish, sprinkle each bowl with spoonfuls of fresh corn kernels, chopped cucumber, diced green pepper, and garlicky croutons.

Each serving contains:
* FIBER: 2 GRAMS • CHOLESTEROL: 0 MILLIGRAMS
* FAT: 10 GRAMS • CALORIES: 216

Mardi Gras
Corn Creole with
Prawns on Parade

Bourbon Street bustles year round, but when Mardi Gras season arrives everyone celebrates. The gumbos are richer, the Creole sauces seem more piquant, and the mint juleps flow. Mardi Gras Corn Creole with Prawns on Parade unmasks the flavors that make Cajun cooking an international favorite. For a French Quarter finale, serve a shimmering, sugar-crusted crème brûlée for dessert.

Makes Six Servings

3 garlic cloves
2 medium onions
2 tablespoons olive oil
1/2 medium green bell pepper, cored, seeded, and
    chopped
1 1/2 cups corn kernels
1/2 cup chopped fresh parsley
6 medium tomatoes, chopped
1/2 cup dry white wine
1 teaspoon sugar
1/2 teaspoon salt
1/2 teaspoon cayenne pepper

1 tablespoon Worcestershire sauce
1/2 teaspoon ground cumin
1/2 teaspoon dried mint
1/2 teaspoon freshly ground black pepper
dash of Tabasco sauce
2 1/2 cups long-grain rice
13 cups water
2 pounds large prawns
1 bay leaf
1/2 lemon

Mince two of the garlic cloves. Reserve a quarter wedge of one onion, and finely chop the rest.

In a large skillet, heat the olive oil at medium temperature. Add the minced garlic, chopped onion, green pepper, and one cup of the corn kernels. Sauté the mixture for two to three minutes.

Add the parsley, tomatoes, wine, sugar, salt, cayenne, Worcestershire, cumin, mint, black pepper, and Tabasco. Mix well to combine. Lower the heat and simmer uncovered for about forty-five minutes, or until the Creole thickens.

While the Creole is simmering, put the rice in a large, lidded saucepan with five cups of water. Add salt to taste, and bring to a boil over a high heat. Cover and simmer for about twenty minutes, until the rice is fluffy.

Meanwhile, prepare the prawns. Bring the remaining eight cups of water to a low boil in a large saucepan. Add the reserved quarter onion, the whole garlic clove, and the bay leaf. Simmer for five minutes.

Add the prawns to the water and simmer about three minutes, or until they are pink but not tightly curled. Drain immediately. As soon as the prawns are cool enough to handle, shell and devein them and set aside.

When the rice is tender, drain it. In a large bowl, toss the rice with the remaining half cup of corn kernels.

Select a large, flamboyant serving platter. Arrange the corn-studded rice in a decorative ring, leaving a space in the middle large enough to hold the corn Creole.

Carefully pour the thickened corn Creole into the center of the ring of rice. Parade the prawns in a circle on top of the rice, and douse them with a mighty squeeze of the lemon. Serve at once.

Each serving contains:

- FIBER: 1 GRAM • CHOLESTEROL: 114 MILLIGRAMS
- FAT: 7 GRAMS • CALORIES: 284

Santa Fe-Style Artichoke Enchiladas with Pipian Sauce

Surprise the most sophisticated crowd with this sensational version of a southwest favorite. The sharp chèvre, although unconventional, is a satisfying complement to the exotically spiced Pipian Sauce. Decorate your table in desert-pastel hues, and select terra cotta bowls for dishes of puréed squash and crisp baby lettuces. Place a tall pitcher of foaming margaritas in the center of the table and get your guests started with hand-blown Mexican goblets rimmed with salt.

Makes Twelve Enchiladas (Serves Six)

ENCHILADAS

> 1 1/2 tablespoons vegetable oil
> 1 1/2 cup corn kernels
> 6 ounces chèvre cheese
> 2 medium dried ancho chilies
> 6 medium-sized artichoke hearts, cooked
> 12 corn tortillas

PIPIAN SAUCE

> 1/2 cup pumpkin seeds
> 2 tablespoons sesame seeds

1/2 cup almonds
1/4 teaspoon whole allspice
4 whole cloves
1/4 teaspoon anise seeds
1/4 teaspoon cumin seeds
1/2 cinnamon stick
2 1/2 tablespoons vegetable oil
1/2 medium onion, chopped
2 garlic cloves, crushed
2 1/2 cups chicken stock
1 teaspoon sugar
1/2 teaspoon salt

Warm the oil in a medium saucepan over medium-low heat. Add the corn kernels and sauté for five minutes. Set aside.

Crumble the chèvre into a small bowl and set aside.

Cover the chilies with hot water, and soak them until they become soft, about five minutes. Drain the chilies, chop them coarsely, and set aside.

Slice each artichoke heart into quarter-inch pieces. Set aside.

To make the sauce, heat a medium skillet over low temperature for several minutes. Add the pumpkin seeds and stir them constantly for four to five minutes, until all the seeds have toasted and popped. Put them in a bowl and set aside.

Reheat the skillet and toast the sesame seeds, stirring constantly, until they become lightly browned. Add them to the pumpkin seeds.

Repeat the process to toast the almonds. Combine them with the other seeds in the bowl.

Using a spice grinder or a mortar and pestle, grind the

allspice, cloves, anise, cumin seeds, and cinnamon. Add them to the seeds and nuts. Mix well and set aside.

Warm one and a half tablespoons of the oil in a skillet over medium heat. Add the onion and garlic and sauté until lightly browned, about five minutes. Add the chilies and continue to sauté for one to two minutes.

Place this mixture, along with the seed mixture, in a food processor or blender. Add one cup of the chicken stock, and blend until the purée is smooth and thick.

Heat the remaining tablespoon of oil in a large saucepan over medium heat. Add the purée and cook, stirring constantly, for about five minutes, until the mixture darkens. Stir in the remaining one and a half cups of stock. Add the sugar and salt, and simmer the sauce over medium-low heat for about ten minutes, stirring occasionally.

Preheat the oven to 350 degrees.

Remove the pan of Pipian Sauce from the stove and arrange all the filling ingredients and the tortillas within easy reach to create the enchiladas.

Spoon out enough of the sauce to cover the bottom of a nine-by-thirteen-inch baking pan.

Dip one of the tortillas in the Pipian Sauce. Let it soak until it becomes soft and coated. Using tongs, transfer the tortilla to the baking pan. Fill it down the center with two tablespoons of the corn kernels, one tablespoon of the artichoke slices, and one tablespoon of chèvre. Roll the tortilla into a tube, and turn it fold-side down in the baking pan. Repeat with the remaining tortillas until they are all stuffed and nestled side by side in the baking pan.

Pour the remaining sauce over the enchiladas, and bake for twenty minutes.

Remove the pan from the oven, garnish the enchiladas with the remaining half cup of corn kernels, and serve hot — either straight from the pan or on individual pottery plates.

Lean Corn Tip: Omit the almonds from the Pipian Sauce.

Each Lean Corn serving contains:

- FIBER: 1.8 GRAMS • CHOLESTEROL: 20 MILLIGRAMS
- FAT: 33 GRAMS • CALORIES: 401

Aztec Onion and Lime Soup with Blue Corn Dumplings

Montezuma, fabled emperor of the Aztecs, might have dined on this zesty soup. It would have been accompanied by corn tortillas covered with a finely woven cotton napkin, and a rich hot chocolate beverage. But why not dress down the presentation to make it perfect for a raucous Super Bowl Sunday? Position your table within yelling distance of the television, and set it with festive placemats and brightly colored napkins. Have an ice cooler nearby filled with bottles of mellow Mexican beer.

Makes Six Servings

ONION SOUP

> 3 tablespoons corn oil
> 4 medium yellow onions, thinly sliced
> 5 garlic cloves, finely chopped
> 2 or 3 serrano chilies, seeded and finely chopped
> 1 large tomato, peeled, seeded, and chopped
> 5 cups chicken stock
> 1/4 cup lime juice
> 1 tablespoon finely grated lime zest
> salt and freshly ground black pepper to taste

DUMPLINGS

> 1 cup blue corn flour
> 2 teaspoons baking powder
> 1 teaspoon salt
> 2 tablespoons vegetable shortening
> 1 egg
> 1/2 cup milk
> 2 tablespoons finely chopped cilantro (fresh
>   coriander) leaves

Over low heat, warm the corn oil in a large heavy pot (preferably one that can be carried to the table). Add the onions and stir to coat them with oil. Cover and cook them slowly for twenty minutes.

Uncover the pot and raise the heat to moderate. Stir in the garlic and chilies and sauté for two minutes. Then add the tomato and continue to cook, stirring, for one more minute.

Add the stock, lime juice and zest, and salt and pepper. Bring the soup to a boil. Lower the heat and simmer, uncovered, for thirty minutes.

Meanwhile, prepare the Blue Corn Dumplings. Sift the corn flour, baking powder, and salt into a medium-sized bowl. Using your fingers, two knives, or a pastry cutter, cut in the vegetable shortening until the mixture resembles fine crumbs.

In a small bowl, beat together the egg and milk. Add the cilantro. Gradually stir the egg mixture into the corn flour mixture, adding only enough of the egg to moisten the flour thoroughly. The dough should not be too wet. Depending on the size of the egg, you may not need to use it all.

When the soup has cooked for thirty minutes, drop the dough into the simmering broth a tablespoon at a time to make about a dozen dumplings. Cover the pot with a tight-fitting lid, and steam the dumplings for fifteen minutes. Keep the soup at a low bubble, and do not lift the lid while the dumplings are cooking.

Bring the cooking pot to the table and serve the soup hot in Mexican-style bowls, with two dumplings floating in each.

Lean Corn Tip: In the dumplings, substitute low-fat milk for the whole milk. Substitute two egg whites for the whole egg.

Each Lean Corn serving contains:

    • FIBER: .8 GRAMS • CHOLESTEROL: 0 MILLIGRAMS
        • FAT: 14.6 GRAMS • CALORIES: 226

Corn Blini Shortstack with Caviar Gorbachev

Fine linen, shimmering silver, and sparkling crystal set the stage for this sophisticated entree. Since "red" means "beautiful" in Russian, the large, pink salmon caviar can be an appropriately lovely alternative to more expensive varieties, such as beluga. Tiny crystal glasses of icy vodka, and perhaps a pot de crème to finish, bring to life the axiom "Living well is the best revenge."

Makes Eighteen Three-Inch Blinis (Serves Six)

1 1/2 cups corn kernels
1 cup milk
1 1/2 cups corn flour
1 1/2 teaspoons baking powder
1/2 teaspoon salt
1/2 teaspoon sugar
2 eggs, separated
1/4 cup vegetable oil
3 tablespoons butter, melted
4 ounces caviar (salmon, beluga, or your favorite
    variety)
1/2 cup sour cream

2 medium red onions, chopped
3 hard-boiled eggs, chopped
3 lemons, cut into wedges
bunch of fresh dill, finely chopped

Place one cup of the corn kernels and the milk in a food processor or blender and purée for three minutes. The mixture should be very smooth.

In a large bowl, sift together the corn flour, baking powder, salt, and sugar. Add the egg yolks, vegetable oil, and pureed corn. Mix until the batter is smooth. Fold in the remaining half cup of corn kernels.

Beat the egg whites until they stand in soft peaks. Fold half of the egg whites gently into the batter with a rubber spatula. Add the remaining egg whites, carefully folding in the mixture toward the center of the bowl.

Heat a skillet or crêpe pan over medium-high heat until it becomes very hot. Lower the heat to medium. Brush the pan with a little of the melted butter, and pour in two tablespoons of the batter. Swirl the pan to form a blin about three inches in diameter. Cook until the batter just sets, about forty-five seconds to a minute. Turn it over and cook on the other side for one minute more.

Remove the blin from the pan and transfer to a low-temperature oven to keep it warm. Prepare the remaining blini, one at a time in the same way, brushing the pan with melted butter as needed.

For an elegant presentation, half fill a medium-sized crystal bowl with shaved ice. Spoon the caviar into a smaller bowl and nestle it to sit firmly in the ice. Fill small individual bowls with the sour cream, onions, hard-boiled eggs, lemon wedges, and dill. Stack the corn blini on a warmed silver salver surrounded by the colorful accompaniments.

Let your guests help themselves by taking a blin, spreading a dab of caviar on top, and adding — as they like — small amounts of their favorite condiments. These blini are made small to be enjoyed as finger food.

Lean Corn Tip: Substitute low-fat milk for the whole milk in the blini batter. Serve with nonfat yogurt instead of sour cream.

Each Lean Corn serving contains:
- FIBER: .6 GRAMS • CHOLESTEROL: 379 MILLIGRAMS
- FAT: 25 GRAMS • CALORIES: 423